EXPERIENCING
the
CROSS

STUDY GUIDE

HENRY BLACKABY

WITH BRIAN SMITH

Multnomah® Publishers *Sisters, Oregon*

EXPERIENCING THE CROSS STUDY GUIDE
published by Multnomah Publishers, Inc.

© 2006 by Henry T. Blackaby
International Standard Book Number: 1-59052-599-X

Unless otherwise indicated, Scripture quotations are from:
The Holy Bible, New King James Version
© 1984 by Thomas Nelson, Inc.
Other Scripture quotations are from:
New American Standard Bible® (NASB) © 1960, 1977, 1995
by the Lockman Foundation. Used by permission.

Multnomah is a trademark of Multnomah Publishers, Inc.,
and is registered in the U.S. Patent and Trademark Office.
The colophon is a trademark of Multnomah Publishers, Inc.

Printed in the United States of America

For information:
MULTNOMAH PUBLISHERS, INC.
601 N. LARCH ST.
SISTERS, OREGON 97759

06 07 08 09 10—10 9 8 7 6 5 4 3 2 1 0

CONTENTS

ABOUT THIS
STUDY GUIDE

The cross of Christ. It's at the very heart of the Christian life. It defines our identity as followers of Jesus. Nothing else is more central. One of Christ's most often repeated commands was to take up one's cross and follow Him.

What does that mean for you? What does the cross reveal about the heart and mind of God? What real differences can a first-century instrument of execution make in the lives of twenty-first-century believers?

We'll discover answers to those and other questions as we examine God's Word through this companion study guide to Dr. Blackaby's book *Experiencing the Cross*.

At the beginning of each lesson you'll find a list of the chapters in *Experiencing the Cross* that correspond to that lesson. We encourage you to read along in his book as you proceed through this study.

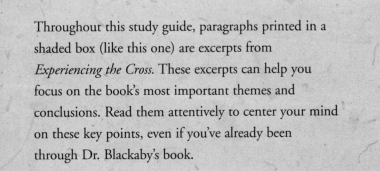

Throughout this study guide, paragraphs printed in a shaded box (like this one) are excerpts from *Experiencing the Cross*. These excerpts can help you focus on the book's most important themes and conclusions. Read them attentively to center your mind on these key points, even if you've already been through Dr. Blackaby's book.

The lessons in this study guide are designed with flexibility to fit a variety of lifestyles. If you have little time to devote to this study and want to get right to the most valuable points in each lesson, focus on the seven Key Questions in each lesson. If you have time to dig deeper, respond to the additional questions after each Key Question, as well as the Scripture passages listed at the end of each lesson under the heading "For Additional Study and Application."

We've also made it easy for you to break each week's study into bite-sized daily portions. They're marked for Days 1 through 5 in each lesson. Then a final section (titled "Experiencing the Cross") will draw each lesson's teaching to a conclusion, guiding you through prayerful reflection ("Reflecting on the Cross") and application of the truth for your daily life ("Changed by the Cross").

Each lesson closes with a Scripture passage for meditation and memorization. In Lesson 1, we've provided practical suggestions for hiding God's Word in your heart.

Finally, don't forget that the Holy Spirit is your Teacher. Start and end with prayer during each study session, and each group discussion if you're going through this study with other believers (see the leader's guide at the end of this book). You can be confident that as you remain open to Him, He will change your mind and your heart by the power of the cross of Christ.

YOUR DESPERATE NEED FOR THE CROSS

*A companion study to the introduction and
chapter 1 in* Experiencing the Cross

LIFE CHANGE OBJECTIVES

It's our prayer that after you have finished this lesson…

* You will begin to open yourself to greater personal ownership and experience of the cross.

* You will grasp more deeply the seriousness of sin— particularly your own sin.

* You will begin to live and speak in ways that will more highly elevate the name of God because of His sacrifice on your behalf.

DAY 1—A BURDEN TO BE SHARED

LESSON

1

DAY

1

When the Lord repeats something, He expects us to sit up and listen! Consider the following statements from the Son of God:

"If anyone desires to come after Me, let him deny himself, and take up his cross daily, and follow Me" (Luke 9:23).

"He who does not take his cross and follow after Me is not worthy of Me" (Matthew 10:38).

"Whoever does not bear his cross and come after Me cannot be My disciple" (Luke 14:27; see also Matthew 16:24; Mark 8:34).

> The cross is not just His; the cross is mine, and the cross is yours. It's an unconditional and uncontestable requirement if we would follow Him as a disciple....
>
> There is nothing more central to the entire Christian life than this theme. It's an absolute essential in the experience of every believer, the very heartbeat of our faith.

Key Question 1

Begin your study of Christ and His cross by talking to Him for a minute or two. Invite Him to change your heart and mind so that you will begin to take ownership of His cross, just as He did so willingly for you. In the space below, write the essence of what you've asked Him to do for you.

Going Deeper

1a. Read again the three passages quoted above (Luke 9:23; Matthew 10:38; Luke 14:27). In your own words, what do these statements say is involved in taking up your cross?

DAY 2—MORE THAN MERE KNOWLEDGE

What does it mean to take up your cross? Throughout this study you'll discover several truths that help answer that question. And underlying everything must be an actual *experience* of the cross.

> No human teacher can open your heart and convince and convict you of the truth of God's Word and how it bears on your life. Only His Spirit can do that. And as He does, you're actually experiencing God; His Word is not simply principles or concepts to increase your head knowledge, but a vehicle for your relationship with the living God, a personal encounter that anchors His truth in the center of your being, equipping and encouraging you to live it from your heart.

LESSON
1

DAY
2

LESSON

1

DAY

2

Key Question 2

• As you embark on your study of the cross, what do you think bearing your cross might cost you?

• What are the reasons you want to bear your cross?

Going Deeper

2a. If possible, describe a time when the sacrifice of Jesus became so real to you that, at least for a time, you lived as a different kind of person.

DAY 3—MORE THAN MERE HISTORY

> Jesus Himself knew and accepted this divine necessity
> of the cross.… The Savior didn't hint that these things
> *might* happen, or even predict that they *would*
> happen—but rather declared that they *must* happen.
> There could be, there would be, no other way.

Key Question 3

Read Matthew 16:21 and Luke 24:44–46. Why is it significant to you
that Jesus recognized there was no other way to fulfill the Father's plan?

Going Deeper

> The cross transcends the physical dimension, and it
> also transcends time. To fully understand it, we must
> see the cross as the whole work of God that began in
> eternity.…

3a. Read Revelation 13:8 and Titus 1:2. Why is it significant
for you that the cross was God's plan throughout the span
of history and beyond?

LESSON

1

DAY

3

DAY 4—THE REASON FOR THE CROSS

LESSON
1

DAY
4

Key Question 4

Read Ephesians 2:11–12 and describe in your own words your prospects apart from the cross of Christ. (Without the cross, how does God view your eternity?)

Going Deeper

4a. Consider the familiar words of John 3:16. Before reading *Experiencing the Cross*, what would you have chosen as the one word that represents the very core of what God is saying in this verse? Why did you choose that word?

> Actually, [the heartbeat of this verse is] the word *perish*....
>   Death is at the very foundation of that statement—eternal death—a destiny that's inescapable by our own efforts.

4b. Describe the daily reminders God has provided all around you to help you understand the seriousness of sin. (See Genesis 3:16–19.)

According to Dr. Blackaby, "the reason we fall short of seeing eternity as God sees it is that we fail to view sin as God views it."

4c. How serious does God know our sin to be? What was the magnitude of the price it required? (See 1 Peter 1:18–19; Hebrews 9:27–28.)

DAY 5—GOD'S RADICAL TREATMENT OF SIN

God knows full well—as we could never know—the appalling destructiveness of sin. He *knows* what sin has done to us; He *knows* how it hurts and impairs us. For every sin we've committed, He understands the full harm done to ourselves and to others, as well as the awful affront that it is to Him. In the cross, therefore, He made complete and total provision for every aspect of what sin has done or ever could do....

God, through the death of His Son, purposed to deal *radically* with sin—not just with our individual sins (plural), but with the sin nature in human beings, with the whole presence of sin (singular), which is the root cause of all our individual sins.

LESSON

1

DAY

5

Our English word *radical* comes from the Latin *radix,* "root." So when Dr. Blackaby says that God planned "to deal radically with sin," he means that God's plan was no mere Band-Aid. His remedy went to the very source from which our individual sins arise.

So consider two scenarios:

Scenario 1: God implements a plan by which He remedies each sin as you commit it, but leaves you essentially unchanged.

Scenario 2: God implements a plan by which He addresses the very root of your sin nature, changing you from the inside out.

Key Question 5

Why is it important to you that God chose the second of these scenarios? (See Ezekiel 36:26–27; John 3:3; Ephesians 4:22–24.)

Going Deeper

5a. Read Hebrews 10:12–17 and describe your eternal prospects after the cross of the sinless Christ has been applied to your life. Under the cross, how does God view your eternity?

CONCLUSION—EXPERIENCING THE CROSS

The seriousness of sin applies not only to your life *before* Christ, but also to your life *in* Christ. In *Experiencing the Cross,* Dr. Blackaby explains that God implemented His plan of spiritual rebirth "for My holy name's sake, which you have profaned among the nations wherever you went. And I will sanctify My great name, which has been profaned among the nations, which you have profaned in their midst; and the nations shall know that I am the LORD…when I am hallowed in you before their eyes" (Ezekiel 36:22–23).

> When Christians today sin consistently, they affect how the world understands God. In fact, they profane His name by their sin. What then should we expect God to do? Doesn't the world today need to see and know that God is holy? Wouldn't God be entirely right and just, therefore, to bring severe affliction upon His people today, so the nations of the world can see His holiness displayed through His discipline of His chosen ones?
>
> As a Christian, destined for heaven, you should take a sober-minded view of your sin.

Key Question 6: Reflecting on the Cross

Take a few minutes and talk with your Father about your life as you have been living it. You might pray something similar to Dr. Blackaby's prayer:

> O God, is there anything in my life, in word or deed, that misrepresents You to people who watch or listen, causing them to take lightly who You are? Are they kept from hearing You because of how I live or what I say? If that's so, I ask You, Lord, to do in me what's necessary to cause them to realize that *You take sin seriously.*

Use the following space to record thoughts that come to mind as you pray with an open heart before Him.

> So whenever you come into God's presence and ask Him, "Why did Jesus have to die? Was there no other way?"—let Him show you from the Scriptures how the cross was necessary for the redemption of the whole world. Then let Him apply that truth to your heart. Let it sink in how it was all *for you*...and exactly what you need.

6a. Take a few minutes more and ask Your Father that question: "Why did Jesus have to die? Was there no other way?" Pray also, "Lord, help me understand more deeply and personally that you did this for me…that it was exactly what I needed."

Use the following space to record your thoughts as you converse with Him.

Key Question 7: Changed by the Cross

Choose one change you will make this week in your thinking, speech, or behavior in order to reflect your gratitude for God's sacrifice on your behalf.

For Meditation and Memorization

In each lesson, we will suggest a key Scripture passage for you to think about throughout the week. Write it on a card and carry it with you. Take it out and read it at least twice each day, reflecting on its significance in your life. This simple process is one way of practicing biblical meditation.

Allow the truth of the passage to sink deeply into your mind and heart. After a few days, you'll probably find that you can remember the specific words. But even if you can't, the essential significance of God's Word will become more deeply embedded in your thinking.

> You were not redeemed with corruptible things, like silver or gold, from your aimless conduct received by tradition from your fathers, but with the precious blood of Christ, as of a lamb without blemish and without spot. (1 Peter 1:18–19)

For Further Study and Application

Each lesson in this book will conclude with a selection of additional Scriptures that you may want to study to strengthen your understanding and application of the Bible's teaching about the cross.

- *The necessity of the cross:* Luke 24:25–26; Acts 4:12; 1 Corinthians 15:3.

- *The seriousness of sin:* Matthew 12:30; Ephesians 2:1–3; Colossians 1:21.

- *The magnitude of Christ's sacrifice on the cross:* Hebrews 7:26; John 1:4.

- *The impact of the cross in our lives:* Romans 5:8–10; Ephesians 2:10.

THE FATHER'S LOVE IN THE CROSS

A companion study to chapters 2–3 in
Experiencing the Cross

LIFE CHANGE OBJECTIVES

It is our prayer that after you have finished this lesson…

- You will be more deeply grateful toward God the Father for His love and sacrifice in the cross.

- You will come away with a greater comprehension of the biblical concept of blood sacrifice—particularly the sacrifice of Christ, to which all others pointed.

- You will enjoy more meaningful worship through the Lord's Supper.

DAY 1—THE FATHER'S PERSONAL INVOLVEMENT

Because it was Jesus Christ, God the Son, whose body was nailed to the cross, we sometimes overlook the activity of God the Father in our salvation. But the whole plan and purpose and implementation of our deliverance from sin is the work of the Father, coming straight from His heart....

From beginning to end in the plan of redemption, God was linked in union with His Son, and in that union, He—God the Father—was actively redeeming a world to Himself.

Key Question 1

Try to read Romans 5:8 and John 3:16 as if you were seeing them for the first time. How did God the Father demonstrate His love for you in the cross?

Going Deeper

1a. In your own words, how does 2 Corinthians 5:18–19 further
clarify the Father's participation in the sacrifice of the cross?

DAY 2—THE FATHER'S GRIEF

From beyond the beginning of time, the Trinity—Father, Son, and
Spirit, all Three—foreknew everything that the cross meant. They all
understood fully the reason for the cross (our sin) and the result of the
cross (our cleansing). And They all felt the pain of the cross to the very
depth of Their infinite being.

> What do you think was on the heart of God, knowing
> that His only Son would become a man so that He
> could take away the sin of the world, suffering such
> cruelty and indignity and shame in the process?…

LESSON

2

Key Question 2

Take a minute or two to consider the question in the preceding
quote, remembering that God did this with *you* in mind. We
encourage you to talk to Him as you think this over. Then write
your response to Dr. Blackaby's question.

DAY

2

LESSON

2

DAY

2

Going Deeper

2a. Carefully read Isaiah 52:13–53:12. As you read, select at least five of
the descriptions of the Messiah's suffering (including, but not limited
to, His physical suffering), and rewrite each one in your own words.

> The final lines in Isaiah 53 contain the whole of the
> gospel of the cross in response to our sin: "He poured
> out His soul unto death, and He was numbered with
> the transgressors, and He bore the sin of many, and
> made intercession for the transgressors" (53:12).
>
> Do you begin to see the magnitude of the love of
> God? When you read John 3:16, it sounds so simple:
> "God so loved the world that He gave His only
> begotten Son." Then you read Isaiah 53—and you see
> that familiar gospel verse through a fresh set of eyes.

2b. Why is it important to you that the Messiah:

…poured out His soul unto death?

…was numbered with the transgressors (sinners)?

…bore the sin of many?

…made intercession for (acted on behalf of) the transgressors?

> It pleased the LORD to bruise Him [or "crush Him," as other translations render it]; He [God the Father] has put Him [His Servant] to grief. (53:10)
>
> It *pleased* the Lord? Yes. This crushing of His Son was actually God's willing, deliberate action, entirely approved and acceptable to Him—and all for you and me.…
>
> There's something in the infinite heart of God that can accept and ordain the cross. What the death of His Son would accomplish somehow outweighed the pain of bringing this about.

LESSON

2

DAY

2

DAY 3—THE MEANING OF CHRIST'S BLOOD

Why all the blood in the Bible? To the casual observer, books such as Leviticus—in which the ritual slaughter and sacrifice of millions of innocent animals is mandated in gory detail—seem morbid.

But this impression fades away when we begin to understand that sin, if left untreated, is fatal and that its cure requires a fatality.

> Sin cannot be dealt with apart from an outpouring of blood. The Father does not forgive sin in any other way....
>
> All the sorrow in the world can never bring forgiveness if we leave out...what God had to do to *be able* to forgive us—yielding His Son to a bloody and absolute death.

Key Question 3

According to Leviticus 17:11 and Deuteronomy 12:23, what is the significance of the blood of a sacrifice? In particular, what does this say about the blood of Christ, poured out for you?

Going Deeper

3a. The world claims that sin can be forgiven in a wide variety of ways. Read Hebrews 9:22. Why is God's remedy for sin so exclusive?

> Blood is required because when God declares the wages of sin is *death*, He means exactly that. What is it that gives us deliverance from this death that we earn because of our sin? Only the lifeblood of the Son of God.

DAY 4—CHRIST'S BLOOD FORESHADOWED

> The death of Jesus Christ was what every previous Passover had always pointed to, and what the slaying of every lamb had foretold. But this time, God Himself was providing the Lamb, and that Lamb was His own Son. His blood would forever cover the life of all who believe in Him, so that their own lives would be passed over by death.

LESSON

2

DAY

4

Key Question 4

In the Old Testament, Israel was given very specific instructions for the Passover animal sacrifice, including the mandate that it be performed repeatedly, year after year. Read some of these instructions in Exodus 12:3–7, 12–14, then read John 1:29, where John the baptist spoke of Jesus. How did the specifics of the Passover sacrifice point to the significance of Jesus' death on the cross?

Going Deeper

4a. How did the cross of Jesus fulfill God's prophecy against Satan in Genesis 3:15?

4b. Throughout the Old Testament, why were so many millions of animals sacrificed year after year at the heart of Israel's system of worship? To find the answer, scan through any of the following chapters: Leviticus 1, 3–4, 7–9, 16–17; Numbers 28–29. Then read Hebrews 9:11–15; 10:1–12.

DAY 5—CHRIST'S BLOOD COMMEMORATED

Have you noticed that every spring the celebrations of Easter and Passover fall close to each other? That's because Jesus was crucified during Passover week nearly two thousand years ago. In fact, Jesus' Last Supper with His disciples was their Passover meal, where Jesus made clear the prophetic connection between Israel's original Passover in Egypt and His own life-saving death. What Israel's annual celebration foreshadowed, the church's ordinance of Communion now commemorates.

> Communion, or the Lord's Supper…is our everlasting memorial until Jesus returns, helping us remember thoroughly and completely the shed blood and the broken body of our Lord as God's provision for us—so we never forget *what* God did and *why.*

Key Question 5

Read for yourself Jesus' words and actions as He instituted the Lord's Supper (Luke 22:7–20 and 1 Corinthians 11:23–26). Next time you celebrate Communion, how will you remind yourself of the Father's sacrificial love through the cross and the significance of Christ's outpoured blood?

LESSON
2

DAY
5

LESSON
2

DAY
5

Going Deeper

5a. What do these two passages reveal about the forward-looking aspects of our Communion celebration?

5b. From now on, how will you worship with a view to the future during Communion?

CONCLUSION—EXPERIENCING THE CROSS

Always in Scripture, it's the Father who purposes and plans and initiates. He works through the Son to accomplish His work, then the Spirit takes what the Father has purposed and brings it into reality in the life of His people.

So it was the Father in His love who purposed our salvation and put together everything about our redemption, and it was the Son through whom the Father accomplished it. And because of what Christ accomplished, you're now born again by the Spirit of God.

The Trinity is one God in three Persons. Each member of the Trinity loves you deeply, gave sacrificially for your salvation, and desires your love and worship in return.

Key Question 6: Reflecting on the Cross

With your Bible open to Isaiah 53, pray to your Father for a few minutes, asking for greater understanding of His sacrifice at the cross. If you aren't sure how to pray, Dr. Blackaby's prayer might serve as a model for you:

> Father, there's no way I could imagine the full meaning
> of these words. But I'm going to ask if somehow, in
> Your grace and in Your mercy, You'll kindly bring me
> to an increasing measure of understanding of what You
> mean in these verses.

As He opens to you greater depths of His heart, write below your insights and your response to Him.

Key Question 7: Changed by the Cross

Choose one way you will remind yourself this week of the Father's love to you, expressed in the cross.

For Meditation and Memorization

But the LORD was pleased to crush Him, putting Him to grief. (Isaiah 53:10, NASB)

For Further Study and Application

- *The Father's participation in the cross:* Matthew 27:45–46 (also Psalm 22:1); Luke 23:44–46; Romans 3:23–26; 8:1–4.

- *The Holy Spirit's application of the cross to your life:* John 3:1–8; Romans 8:8–17.

- *Jesus' blood foreshadowed in the Old Testament:* Genesis 8:18–9:6; 22:1–18; 2 Chronicles 29–30, 35 (two revivals in Israel, each after many years of disobedience).

- *Other perspectives on the Lord's Supper:* Matthew 26:17–30; Mark 14:12–26

THE SON'S OBEDIENCE IN THE CROSS

A companion study to the Part Two introduction and chapters 4–5
in Experiencing the Cross

LIFE CHANGE OBJECTIVES

It is our prayer that after you have finished this lesson…

- You will have gained a fresh comprehension of the Son's complete obedience to the Father.

- You will value more highly the role of suffering and humility in your "education" toward obedience.

- You will experience deeper awe, gratitude, and worship as you contemplate the darkness and depth of the death Christ died— the death we deserved.

DAY 1—THE SON'S ABSOLUTE SUBMISSION

Can you imagine a child who lives every day of his life in perfect obedience to his parents? There is no such child on earth today, but there was one living on earth two thousand years ago.

Can you imagine an adult—even a Christian, like you, who knows God as Father—who conducts his or her life absolutely without sin, in unshakeable, full obedience to God? Again, no such person exists. Except the One who lived more than a decade as a flesh-and-blood adult, facing all the same temptations and hardships that we face.

Key Question 1

In your own words, describe Jesus' mindset (or describe His conduct throughout a typical day), in light of His words in John 5:30; Matthew 26:39, 42, 44.

> Jesus learned what was on the Father's heart, then implemented it, living it out in flesh-and-blood reality, though His path to obedience was not an easy one.

LESSON

3

Going Deeper

1a. Look closely at the way Jesus worded the prediction of His impending suffering in Luke 9:22. How did this reflect His anticipation of His future obedience?

DAY

1

1b. Jesus flowed immediately from the prediction of His death into the teaching of Luke 9:23–26. What was He saying to you about following His example of absolute obedience?

DAY 2—THE SON'S CLASSROOM

Not only did Jesus' obedience lead Him into suffering, but the Bible tells us that suffering also led Him into greater obedience.

Key Question 2
According to each of the following astounding Scripture passages, how did suffering prepare the sinless Jesus for His work on our behalf?

Hebrews 5:7–10

Hebrews 2:9–10

Hebrews 2:17–18

> Jesus allowed His suffering to keep moving Him forward on the pathway of conformity to the Father's will; He let obedience be the direct result of all His suffering....
>
> Jesus in His obedient manhood was made perfect—made complete in everything God required in the Savior. As a result, He became the perfect provision God was looking for, the spotless Lamb of God who takes away the sin of the world by His sacrificial death.

Going Deeper

2a. Although we will never live perfectly in this life, how do we follow Christ's example in coming ever closer to that goal? (See James 1:2–4; 1 Peter 1:7–9.)

DAY 3—THE SON'S RELINQUISHED PRIVILEGE

> To yield this way in suffering obedience to the Father's will meant that Jesus had to totally give up His personal rights.... Jesus gave Himself over to God, to learn and do His Father's will.

LESSON
3

DAY
3

Throughout His earthly life and His death, Jesus never ceased to be God, and He never ceased to deserve all the privilege that had been His throughout eternity past. What He forfeited, He forfeited voluntarily. Gladly.

Key Question 3
What were some of the genuine rights that Jesus gave up on your behalf?

Matthew 4:1–11

Matthew 26:50–57

Philippians 2:6–8

Going Deeper

3a. In light of Jesus' attitude, how does God call you to live a typical day in your life? (See Philippians 2:3–5.) Describe specific things you would do or not do as you obey this teaching.

> Taking up your cross—living by the cross of Christ—
> means no more rights.

3b. God calls us to relinquish "rights" that we never deserved. How can you learn to do this gladly, every day, as a gesture of gratitude for the One who willingly relinquished rights He *did* deserve?

DAY 4—THE SON FACED THE ABYSS

In several Scripture passages, we see both Jesus and Paul referring to physical death as "sleep" (Mark 5:39; John 11:11; 1 Corinthians 11:30; 15:18, 51), as though there were something temporary or incomplete about it. But when Jesus at Gethsemane told His disciples, "My soul is exceedingly sorrowful, even to death" (Matthew 26:38)…

LESSON

3

DAY

4

I believe He meant this literally.

In the struggle He was entering upon, I believe our Savior came right on the edge of death....

He was not talking about physical death; He was facing something else, something far more profound and overwhelming than anything the martyrs ever faced. Gathering over the soul of our Savior, deepest darkness and a midnight of desolation was about to descend....

It appears that our Lord, in this garden, began to actually experience the first wave of suffering and sorrow that would soon engulf Him. In that moment, a sense of utter desolation washed over Him—a sense of homelessness, I believe, more intense than anything we can conceive of.

Jesus foresaw the full implications of the death He would die.

Key Question 4

Read Isaiah 53:3; Luke 22:41–44; Matthew 26:37–38; 27:45–46. Watch for the intensity of Jesus' emotional response to the fate He willingly accepted. Describe this death in your own words.

Going Deeper

4a. Why do you have reason to celebrate as you face physical death? (See 1 Corinthians 15:54–58.)

DAY 5—THE SON RANSOMED THE CONDEMNED

We've all heard stories of heroes who pushed someone out of the path of a speeding vehicle, only to be struck and killed themselves. We rightly honor such selfless individuals.

But consider the doom we deserved. Consider how fully we deserved it. And consider the incredible love of the One who accepted it in order that we might not have to.

> The inevitable casting into outer darkness that God had warned in Scripture would happen to all who do not believe, a darkness utterly void of life and light—this is what was descending upon the soul of our Savior. An outer darkness where there is weeping and wailing and gnashing of teeth—this was the pathway our Savior walked. He passed that way in our place, so that you and I need never walk that way ourselves.
>
> And it was all utterly real. This was the essence of death…and it lies at the very heart of the gospel.

LESSON

3

DAY

5

LESSON
3

DAY
5

Key Question 5
Unpack the good news that is packed in such simple words as "Christ died for our sins" (1 Corinthians 15:3). What are its deeper implications? (See also John 11:25–26.)

Going Deeper

5a. In light of these insights, next time you explain the gospel to someone, how will you present it differently than you have before? Consider not only your words, but the manner in which you share.

> This deeper death is the death Jesus died, and according to His own promise it's also the kind of death He has saved you and me *from*....
>
> Jesus did not just fall asleep; He actually *died*—in the most absolute way possible. And it was your sin and mine that gave to His death that deepest, darkest dimension.

CONCLUSION—EXPERIENCING THE CROSS

Key Question 6: Reflecting on the Cross
Think back over the realities you've seen as you've worked through this lesson. Talk them over with the Lord for a few minutes. If you're not sure how to pray, here are some of the words you might use:

"Jesus, there is no way I can comprehend the fullest significance of Your death. But I am capable of minimizing it and thereby dishonoring You. Please increase my understanding of Your sacrifice on my behalf. Show me how to answer the question, 'What is true death?' And as I come to a deeper appreciation of Your complete obedience, give me wisdom and resolve to follow Your example, whatever the cost. May my heart be filled to overflowing with love for You, in response to the amazing love You have shown to me."

As you pray, write below any new insights you gain, or changes you think God wants you to make in your thinking, speech, or behavior.

Key Question 7: Changed by the Cross
Choose one tangible way to express gratitude to your Savior for the death He died on your behalf. How will it affect the way you live this next week?

For Meditation and Memorization

I do not seek My own will but the will of the Father who sent Me. (John 5:30b)

For Further Study and Application

- *Jesus' complete obedience:* Mark 14:36; John 5:17–21; 15:10; 17:1–8.

- *Our growth toward obedience through hardship:* 2 Corinthians 4:7–18; 11:23–12:10; Philippians 3:7–17.

- *The profound difference between physical and spiritual death:* Mark 5:39; John 3:36; 5:24; 11:11; 1 Corinthians 11:28–30; 15:12–53; Revelation 2:11; 20:6, 14–15; 21:6–8.

THE WORK ACCOMPLISHED ON THE CROSS

A companion study to chapters 6–7 in
Experiencing the Cross

LIFE CHANGE OBJECTIVES

It is our prayer that after you have finished this lesson...

- You will comprehend in greater depth the incredible exchange—
  our sin for Christ's righteousness.

- You will experience a deeper hatred toward sin through a closer
  identification with the cross.

- You will celebrate the victorious completion and confirmation of
  God's salvation in the resurrection of Jesus.

DAY 1—CHRIST MADE SIN

LESSON
4

DAY
1

When the Son of God came to earth, He came to do a job, to complete an assignment. Part of the assignment took Him thirty-some years to complete.

But His greatest and most difficult work was to subject Himself to an appalling, miraculous exchange that would change our eternal destiny. He went to the cross, and there the first half of the exchange took place: God the Father "made Him who knew no sin to be sin for us" (2 Corinthians 5:21).

Christ actually *became* sin for us. What a thought!

Language fails us here. Our minds grope to understand what finite minds can never understand. As I have placed my heart and mind into the Scriptures, seeking to better comprehend the death of Christ for our sins, I've been staggered by the immensity and enormity of this truth....

Jesus—the One who knew no sin, the One who had *never* sinned—was *made the essence of sin* for us, all by the deliberate action and purpose of God the Father.

Take a moment and carefully reread Dr. Blackaby's words above. Then ask your Father to open your mind and heart to the horror and joy of Christ made sin.

Key Question 1

Paraphrase each of the following passages, keeping in mind that each one is a portrayal of the sinless Christ being made sin.

Matthew 27:45–46

1 Peter 2:24

1 Peter 3:18

Going Deeper

1a. How would you explain the concept of "Christ made sin" to someone who had never heard or read anything from the Bible?

LESSON
4

DAY
1

DAY 2—THE WHOLE WORLD'S SIN

LESSON
4

DAY
2

"God so loved the world…" (John 3:16). Throughout history, God's plan has been a global one. That's why Jesus paid a global price.

> Upon the Savior, upon His beloved Son, God placed "the sin *of the world*" (John 1:29). Whom does that include? All people throughout all time, from the days of Genesis, down through the centuries of human history, and continuing into all the future of human existence on earth, however short or long that may be.

Because Jesus accepted half of the great exchange on the cross, becoming the essence of sin, anyone who places faith in Him will receive access to the second half of the exchange.

Key Question 2

What are some of the incredible benefits we can receive because Christ took our sin on Himself?

2 Corinthians 5:18–21

Romans 5:9

Romans 6:23

Going Deeper

2a. You've examined the miracle of Christ made sin. Imagine you're talking to someone who knows nothing of the Bible. How would you explain the equally miraculous transaction by which you can be made the righteousness of God in Christ?

DAY 3—UNITED WITH CHRIST
AGAINST SIN

Our whole identity with Christ is found in the cross. It was there that God dealt totally and radically with sin. And it's there that God intends for us to be so united with Christ in His death that we will forever *hate* sin, *abhor* sin, and *forsake* sin. In our intimate relationship with Christ in His crucifixion, God intends for us to see sin as He does, and to *feel the horrors of sin as Christ did*—and to therefore let the Father crucify sin in our lives just as He crucified His own Son. He wants us to literally die to sin, never again to know it as a way of life....

LESSON
4

DAY
3

LESSON
4

DAY
3

When we truly consider that utter desolation of soul and spirit, that blackness of homelessness that came over our Savior because of our sin, it creates within us an intensity *against* sin. And when this intensity burns in our heart, the result is personal holiness.

Key Question 3

What does it mean in your day-to-day existence that you've been "crucified with Christ" and that you're "dead to sin"? (See Romans 6:6–7, 11–12; Galatians 2:20.)

Going Deeper

3a. Explain Dr. Blackaby's statement above: "Our whole identity with Christ is found in the cross."

3b. Describe one or two specific ways you'd like to see the exchange of your sin for God's righteousness working itself out in your life.

DAY 4—JESUS' QUIET CONFIDENCE

During the ordeal of Jesus' series of trials on trumped-up charges, His silence puzzled His interrogators and accusers

Most of us, when falsely accused, would try to vindicate our innocence, but Jesus did not. Why do you suppose He responded this way? Why would He keep quiet?

We find the answer when we see this moment from God's perspective. Jesus sought approval from One and One only: His Father in heaven. And He knew that before God, He was absolutely innocent. So why bother discussing or defending it with men? Why waste words? Why play their game? As long as God knows—that's enough.

What is more, Jesus knew that because He was indeed absolutely innocent of *any* sin, His death would not be the conclusion of the event of the cross.

LESSON
4

DAY
4

LESSON

4

DAY

4

Jesus grasped fully the message and the promise of Scripture. And because He trusted His Father and remained yielded and obedient to His will, He knew that death—even deepest death—would not be the end of the story.

Key Question 4

Based on each of the following passages, what did Jesus know about the rest of the story beyond His death?

Isaiah 53:10–12 (a passage Jesus would have often reflected upon)

Luke 24:46

Hebrews 12:2

Going Deeper

4a. Read 1 Peter 2:21–25. What does Jesus' quiet confidence reveal about His relationship with His Father?

4b. In what situations might you draw upon the same confidence that Jesus did when He "committed Himself to Him who judges righteously"?

DAY 5—THE COMPLETION OF THE CROSS

The necessity of Jesus' resurrection was as certain in His mind as was the necessity of His death.

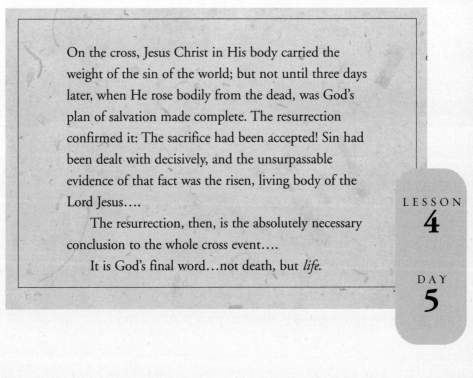

On the cross, Jesus Christ in His body carried the weight of the sin of the world; but not until three days later, when He rose bodily from the dead, was God's plan of salvation made complete. The resurrection confirmed it: The sacrifice had been accepted! Sin had been dealt with decisively, and the unsurpassable evidence of that fact was the risen, living body of the Lord Jesus....

The resurrection, then, is the absolutely necessary conclusion to the whole cross event....

It is God's final word...not death, but *life*.

LESSON
4

DAY
5

LESSON

4

DAY

5

Key Question 5

Why are your life's meaning and your eternal destiny critically dependent on the resurrection of Jesus from the dead? (See Matthew 28:1–10, 16–20; 1 Corinthians 15:12–26.)

Going Deeper

> He knew His death was a "must."
> But so was rising from the dead.
> And so was His ascension into glory.

5a. In Revelation 5:6–14 we see the scene of Jesus' eternal glorification in heaven. How can you draw upon the truth of His resurrection to make a small part of that scene true here on earth?

CONCLUSION—EXPERIENCING THE CROSS

Jesus' work on the cross is finished. He completed the first half of the great exchange, becoming sin on our behalf. And because He was guilty of no sin, He conquered sin and death and rose to life, confirming the acceptability of His sacrifice and living now to receive glory on earth and in heaven.

But the potential impact of Jesus' finished work is still being realized. Many have not yet received the second half of the exchange, by which a sinful human becomes the righteousness of God in Christ. And many Christians are not taking full advantage of the power of Christ's resurrection in order to bring Him glory through a supernaturally obedient life.

> Remember the old gospel song, "Jesus paid it *all*, all to Him I owe"? Jesus indeed paid it *all*, and therefore I owe Him everything.

Key Question 6: Reflecting on the Cross

Scan back over the insights you've gained from this lesson, and then turn your heart toward the Lord. Invite Him to further His ongoing work in your life. The following prayer is one way you might ask Him to do this:

"Father, I'm grateful for the amazing exchange of my sin for Your righteousness, all made possible through the cross of Christ. Help me identify more and more closely with the cross, so that I abhor sin more strongly and so that I allow Your righteousness in me to become more and more evident in my conduct. Thank You that Jesus is alive today to glorify Himself through my life. Help me draw more upon the power of His resurrection for the purpose of Your glory."

Use the following space to write any thoughts that come to mind as you pray.

Key Question 7: Changed by the Cross

Choose one specific way you will live this week in closer identification with the cross and its completed work.

For Meditation and Memorization

> He made Him who knew no sin to be sin for us, that we
> might become the righteousness of God in Him.
> (2 Corinthians 5:21)

For Further Study and Application

- *The exchange of our sin for God's righteousness in Christ:* Romans 5:17–21; Galatians 3:13; Philippians 3:8–14; Hebrews 10:19–22.

- *Our identity in the cross:* Galatians 6:14; 1 Corinthians 2:1–5.

- *Jesus perspective on life beyond His death:* John 2:19–22; 10:17–18; 17:5; Acts 2:32

- *The significance of Jesus' resurrection:* Luke 24; John 16:7–33; John 20–21; Acts 1:1–3; 1 Corinthians 15:27–58.

NEW DOORS OPENED BY THE CROSS

A companion study to the Part Three introduction and chapters 8–11 in Experiencing the Cross

LIFE CHANGE OBJECTIVES

It is our prayer that after you have finished this lesson…

- You will take personal ownership of Christ's death and resurrection in such a way that you will experience true, radical life change.

- You will begin to tap into all of the blessings, power, and other resources released by the cross.

- You will engage in spiritual warfare with a mindset of accomplished victory.

DAY 1—THE DOOR TO GENUINE TRANSFORMATION

"If anyone is in Christ, he is a new creation; old things have passed away; behold, all things have become new" (2 Corinthians 5:17). Do you really believe this bold declaration? Many Christians tragically fail God and themselves because they don't.

Being "in Christ," Paul says, means having *all* things become *new*. Everything is transformed. You're a *new* creation.

This change is huge; no transformation can possibly be greater. You go from being condemned to being forgiven. You go from irremovable guilt to being declared righteous by God—not because of your own righteousness, but because you've opened your life to receive Christ and *His* righteousness. And when God looks at you—wonder of wonders—He no longer sees your sin but the righteousness of His own Son.

If then you've been born again, if you've been redeemed and delivered through that transaction by faith, isn't it reasonable to expect that everyone around you would be able to see the evidence of it? Simply by watching your life, shouldn't the world be able to see the reality of what God accomplished in the cross?

Key Question 1

- If you are convinced you are a new creation, describe the evidence that your life has been transformed.

- If you find that you have trouble believing that you are truly and completely *new,* what is it that seems to be giving you this trouble? (You may need to invite the Lord to help you answer this question. See Psalm 139:23–24 for a suggested prayer.)

Going Deeper

1a. What is the real difference between the one who has life and the one who doesn't? (See 1 John 5:11–12. Answer in terms of observable behavior.)

LESSON
5

DAY
1

DAY 2—THE DOOR TO INTIMATE RELATIONSHIP

Maybe we *think* we're living a transformed life. We say the right words and make the right moves, but there's no substantial reality to back them up.

> We all have difficulty sometimes in remembering the difference between experiencing a true relationship with the God of our salvation and experiencing merely the practice of religion. We can practice everything correctly, do all the "spiritual" things people expect us to do, but never progress in...the close, intimate walk with God that is so essential for true transformation.

Key Question 2

What does each of the following passages mean if it's to be taken at face value (rather than as merely abstract or symbolic)?

2 Corinthians 5:14–15

Galatians 2:20

Going Deeper

2a. If you're married or have a boyfriend or girlfriend, how much would you enjoy the relationship if you treated it as an abstract idea, not a tangible reality?

The cross isn't a doctrine to be discussed, but a fact [and a relationship] to be experienced.

DAY 3—THE DOOR TO NEW LIFE

According to Scripture, a Christian has *actually, genuinely* participated with Christ in both His death and His resurrection. We saw these ideas on Day 2, and we'll examine them in greater depth in Lesson 7, but let's catch one more preliminary glimpse of them in order to begin absorbing their experiential truth.

LESSON
5

DAY
3

Key Question 3

Read Romans 6:3–11 carefully. Try to set aside any rationalizing and minimizing, and just let God speak. In your own words, what does it mean to die and be raised with Christ?

Going Deeper

I'm sure most of those who watched [Mel Gibson's film *The Passion of the Christ*] had great sympathy with Jesus, but I doubt many of us sensed that we were up there on that cross, crucified and bleeding with Him. Yet I believe you and I are also called to begin understanding those depths....

When Paul stated in 2 Corinthians that anyone in Christ is a "new creation," with all things becoming new in their lives, the newness he referred to was the living presence of Christ Himself. That's what's new (and *stays* new) in our lives when we live by the cross.

3a. What does this intense connection with Christ imply about our personal relationship with Him?

DAY 4 — THE DOOR TO COMPLETE PROVISION

> ...the cross has procured for us unimaginable riches and blessings from God the Father....
>
> The truth of the crucified Christ includes *everything* we could ever truly need....
>
> In our union with Christ Jesus, we're *complete*. So often we think, *I still lack something*. Our problem is one of belief. We haven't yet grasped the truth that God accomplished all that He says He accomplished in the cross.

Key Question 4

Choose at least two of the following passages and describe the benefits that the cross releases to us.

Romans 8:32

Ephesians 1:3–5

Colossians 2:9–10

LESSON

5

DAY

4

LESSON

5

DAY

4

2 Peter 1:2–4

Romans 8:28

Hebrews 4:16; 10:19–22

Going Deeper

> Knowing He has provided for us so completely
> through the cross, imagine how greatly dishonoring it
> is to Him when we set all that aside and try to
> function instead in the flesh.

4a. Can you identify one way in which you're trying to do on your own what you can do only by means of God's provision? If so, how will you start depending on His provision?

DAY 5—THE DOOR TO CONFIDENT VICTORY

On the cross, Christ accomplished absolute victory over Satan so that we never need to live in spiritual defeat. Satan is a liar (John 8:44) who tries to make us doubt Christ's victory. But if we fill our minds and hearts with the truth, we'll live confidently in the triumph that is already ours.

Key Question 5

Consider all the forces fighting against us, as described in Colossians 2:13–15 and Romans 8:32–39. Why is the sacrifice of Christ sufficient to conquer them all?

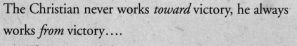

> The Christian never works *toward* victory, he always works *from* victory....
>
> The cross and the resurrection brought about the complete, total defeat of evil in any and every form....
>
> *God* is...*for* us—and therefore who can be against us? Absolutely no one. No one in the heavens. No one on earth. No one in hell.

LESSON
5

DAY
5

LESSON

5

DAY

5

Going Deeper

5a. How does Hebrews 10:12–14 explain the connection between our salvation and Christ's defeat of His enemies? How is this real for you?

CONCLUSION—EXPERIENCING THE CROSS

When you invite God to apply the cross to your life, He makes available "all things that pertain to life and godliness" (2 Peter 1:3; see also Romans 8:32).

> Are you letting God define for you what He means by "all things"? Or are you somehow limiting God? "All things" is a phrase that you don't really get a handle on unless you meditate deeply on it in God's presence.

In our efforts to understand and receive "all things," God has given us a Helper, the Holy Spirit:

...persuading us to ask specifically for that which God has already richly provided for us through the cross of Christ. That's the work of the Holy Spirit—to help us ask as we should, because "we do not know what we should pray for as we ought" (Romans 8:26).

Key Question 6: Reflecting on the Cross

So why not start asking now? Maybe Dr. Blackaby's prayer will help you.

"O Father in heaven, I know Your promises. I know You have made available everything I need to live a godly life—I know that all this is already mine. And yet I just don't fully grasp how to implement these blessings. *But if You'll show me, I will respond.*"

If you do that continually over a lifetime, you'll increasingly become all that God wants you to be, as His grace and peace are multiplied unto you.

Use the space below to write any thoughts that come to mind as you pray.

Key Question 7: Changed by the Cross

Choose one way you will live differently this week, knowing that you are a new creation, living from accomplished victory, having your every need already provided.

For Meditation and Memorization

He who did not spare His own Son, but delivered Him up for us all, how shall He not with Him also freely give us all things? (Romans 8:32)

For Further Study and Application

- *Genuinely changed by the cross:* Galatians 2:19–21; 1 Corinthians 1:17–24; 2:1–5.

- *Complete provision through the cross:* John 1:16; 1 Corinthians 3:21–23.

- *Praying for God's blessings and provision:* John 16:23; 1 Corinthians 2:9–12.

- *Christ's complete victory over Satan:* Ephesians 1:19–22; 6:10–13; Colossians 2:10.

VIEWING SIN IN LIGHT OF THE CROSS

A companion study to chapters 12–13 in
Experiencing the Cross

LIFE CHANGE OBJECTIVES

It is our prayer that after you have finished this lesson…

- You will have a stronger abhorrence of sin.

- You will enter into a new level of submission to God's sanctifying work in your life.

- You will actively cooperate with God's sanctifying work by repenting whenever you become conscious of sin in you.

DAY 1—SIN: THE SOLE REASON
FOR THE CROSS

The purpose for the cross is simple. And horrific in its ugly simplicity.

> *The cross of Christ has to do exclusively with sin;* that's why it's a part of history!

If the cross is about sin—and sin alone—then imagine what its focus must be when applied to our lives. The cross is not simply a trinket we hang around our necks. It's not just a pattern embroidered on our Bible covers. It's not merely a symbol by which people recognize our places of worship.

The cross is a tool of execution intended for the guilty. It's an instrument for eradicating sin at its root.

> If you more fully understand the meaning of the cross, you realize that to take up our cross as Jesus tells us to means that you deliberately choose to radically deal with sin in your life....
>
> ...as God dealt with sin in the cross, He dealt with it *radically*. How could it be less in our lives? God doesn't deal thoroughly with sin on the cross and then just barely touch sin in your life.

Key Question 1

In light of what you've just read, now read the broader context of two of Jesus' "take up your cross" teachings: Mark 8:31–38; 10:17–27 (see also Matthew 16:21–26; Luke 9:22–26). What specific dealings with sin might be required of you as you take up your cross and follow Christ?

Going Deeper

1a. Why is it good news that the focus of the cross is on sin? Why is this good news for you?

DAY 2—SIN AND THE DISCIPLE

Key Question 2

Study two more of Jesus' "take up your cross" teachings: Matthew 10:38; Luke 14:27. Why isn't a person who is unwilling to confront his own sin worthy to be a disciple of Christ?

LESSON

6

DAY

2

LESSON

6

DAY

2

It's unthinkable to say, "Father, thank You for laying the sin of the world on Your Son…but please don't talk to me about sin in my life. I just want to have the joy of following You."…

…it's time for us to let the living Christ once again define the terms of discipleship. The essence of a follower of Jesus Christ is one who has dealt with and continually deals with sin in a radical manner in his or her life.

Going Deeper

2a. What, then, are the options facing a person who wants to keep his or her sin and also wants to be a disciple of Christ?

2b. Are being a disciple of Christ and being a believer in Christ the same thing? If not, how are they different?

2c. If being a disciple and a believer are different, why would it be important to be both?

DAY 3—THE DEADLY SERIOUSNESS OF SIN

> God wasn't playing games with sin when He allowed His Son to be crucified. Sin is as bad as God tells us it is, with eternal consequences every bit as horrible as God describes them. We must never forget: Sin is so serious to the mind of God that He was willing to take His only Son—who knew no sin and lived in perfect holiness—and to *make* Him to be sin for us.

Recall our earlier study of the message behind all the Old Testament sacrificial bloodshed—namely, that *sin requires a fatality.* As Dr. Blackaby writes, "Death is sin's payoff." Always.

LESSON
6

DAY
3

Sin is deadly serious to God.

Does that deadliness hold for Christians as well as for unbelievers? Absolutely! The soul that continues to sin will know the withering and dying of a relationship with God, and a shrinking capacity to receive and enjoy His purpose and will.

Key Question 3

Wherever you might be in relationship to God, it is absolutely necessary that you take sin as seriously as God does. If you don't, what consequences might result in your life circumstances? (See Genesis 2:16–17; Acts 5:1–5; Romans 6:23; James 1:15; 5:19–20.)

Going Deeper

By the very nature of God's absolute holiness He *must* confront your sin. He cannot overlook it, nor will He; His holy nature demands that He deal with it. He has an utter hatred of sin that is absolute and irreversible, and this is true of *every* sin in our lives.

3a. Have you come face–to-face with God's inevitable confrontation of your sin? Or are you living in denial? What attitudes and actions on your part would make this confrontation a gain rather than a loss? (See 1 Corinthians 11:27–29; 1 John 1:9; Matthew 3:8.)

DAY 4—WHAT SIN IS AND DOES

> All sin is deadly, and the deadening effect of our own sin goes beyond ourselves....
>
> You can never sin in private. You may be able to sin in secret, but you can't in private, because your sin will immediately affect everything around you. Your church, your family, your work—everything will to some degree be put out of joint because of your sin.

Key Question 4

Read Genesis 3:16–19; Romans 8:20–22; Joshua 7:1–26. How might other people, and even the natural world, suffer consequences from your sin? (Think specifically about those your life touches.)

LESSON

6

DAY

4

Going Deeper

4a. Read 1 John 3:4, and explain John's definition of sin in your own words.

Don't get hung up on the mistaken idea that "law" always means legalism. In the verse you just studied, John was writing to Christians in the age of grace. In this context, "law" simply means the revealed standards of God, based on His character. Those have remained forever the same, throughout both the Old Testament and the New, and they will always be the same. God never changes (Malachi 3:6; James 1:17).

4b. How can you remedy ignorance of or rebellion against God's law in your own life? (See Psalm 119:11; 2 Timothy 3:16–17.)

> The practicing sinner is lawless, without God's law. In other words, it means you're trying to live without any standard of God's Word to judge your decisions. You're living outside the clear directives of His Word.

DAY 5—WHAT SIN REQUIRES OF US

Repeatedly in Scripture, we read that sin requires our repentance. But what does it mean to repent?

> Repentance is acknowledging that what I've done is serious to God, that in some area of life I've actually been going in an opposite direction from where He wants me to go, and my direction is a wrong one. So I make a choice—a conscious choice—to turn around and go in *His* direction, because Jesus Christ is the *way* and the truth and the life. I flee to the Savior and ask Him to help me live in a way that's the opposite of how I've been living.

Key Question 5
How does each of the following passages help you further define and understand repentance?

Luke 3:7–14

Acts 26:20

LESSON
6

DAY
5

LESSON
6

DAY
5

2 Corinthians 7:8–11

Revelation 2:4–5

Going Deeper

> Just as our sin affects those around us, so also our getting right with God will have tremendously positive effects all around us. A step of repentance and obedience can be the tremor that brings a huge movement of God and great freedom and release to many.

5a. Consider the ways that your sin might be hurting or holding back others around you. How might your repentance positively impact the lives of many others? (Be specific. You don't need to write your response if it's too sensitive, but you do need to answer before God.)

CONCLUSION—EXPERIENCING THE CROSS

If God in this moment is bringing some sin to mind
and the Holy Spirit is convicting your heart, there's
only one way to deal with it. There must be *repentance*.
Just asking God to forgive you isn't enough.

Repentance means action. It means turning around...abandoning your old, sinful direction and launching out in a new, obedient direction.

Key Question 6: Reflecting on the Cross

Take some time now to open your heart before God. Invite Him to help you see your own sin clearly, understand its devastating impact, humbly confess it, and willingly repent (go the other way). You might want to pray something like this:

"Lord, make me sensitive to my own sin. It is my sin that crucified my Savior, and my sin has caused nothing but destruction in my life and the lives of others. I agree with You about my sins. [That's confession. Speak specifically to Him about your sins.] In this moment I repent in my mind and heart. And I commit to repent promptly in action as well. [Tell Him what you are committing to do.] By the power of Your Spirit living in me, give me the strength and will to live now for You."

In the following space, record a summary of your prayer and any thoughts that come to mind as you pray.

Key Question 7: Changed by the Cross

What is one step of action you will take this week as part of your repentance from sin?

For Meditation and Memorization

> For the wages of sin is death, but the gift of God is eternal life in Christ Jesus our Lord. (Romans 6:23)

For Further Study and Application

- *Christ's disciple must deal with sin:* John 8:31–32; Romans 6:14; 1 Corinthians 11:24–29.

- *The nature and consequences of sin:* Jeremiah 31:30; Ezekiel 18:20.

- *Repentance from sin:* Romans 2:2–6; 2 Peter 3:7–9; Revelation 3:15–20.

LIVING IN THE POWER OF THE CROSS

A companion study to chapters 14—15 in
Experiencing the Cross

LIFE CHANGE OBJECTIVES

It is our prayer that after you have finished this lesson…

- You will understand better how to live out your participation in Christ's death and resurrection.

- You will understand how to listen to the Spirit's conviction concerning sin.

- You will recognize the cross's power in your supernatural daily living; or, if you don't see the cross's power in your life, you will reexamine your faith and your understanding of the cross.

DAY 1—CRUCIFIED WITH CHRIST

Different Christians respond differently to the word *mystical.* Tragically, many wrongs have been perpetrated in the name of "Christian mysticism," when teachings have clearly violated God's revealed truth. The follower of Christ must exercise discernment.

But at the same time, Scripture presents us with numerous truths that our limited minds can never understand or explain completely. In that sense, such truths are indeed *mystical.* When we claim to have full understanding of these realities, we are either making too little of God or making too much of ourselves, or both.

The doctrine of our actual participation with Christ in His death and His resurrection has a mystical aspect to it. Yet is *true truth.* We can't know it exhaustively, but we can gain genuine knowledge about it. We can't explain every detail of its workings, but we can—we *must*— experience and live out its reality.

This is at the heart of our experience of the cross.

> Effective faith...understands that when we enter a relationship with Jesus Christ, we're *immersed* into His death and into His burial....
>
> Our immersion into Christ's death and burial is so complete that Paul tells us we actually "died to sin" (Romans 6:2).

Key Question 1

Read carefully through Romans 6, paying special attention to Paul's teaching about our union with Christ in His death. (We'll do the same with His resurrection on Day 3.) In a few sentences, summarize the reality of our death with Christ.

Going Deeper

1a. What does each of the following passages add to your understanding of your death with Christ?

Galatians 2:20

2 Corinthians 5:14–15

1 Peter 2:24

LESSON
7

DAY 2—FREED FROM SIN

Our union with Christ in His crucifixion isn't just an idea outside of ourselves, but a real change inside us.

DAY
2

LESSON

7

DAY

2

The cross deals not only with the *penalty* for our sins, the cross also overcomes the whole reality of our nature of sin. It is this nature that brings about specific sinful actions and attitudes in our lives. We can be assured that if the cross dealt radically with *sin* then the cross will also deal radically with *sins*....

We die to sin as the dominating factor in our behavior. In every area where we experience moral failure and addiction and defeat, in every area where we simply cannot help ourselves, we can now find absolute, radical victory over sin.

Key Question 2

How does each of the following passages describe the real changes in you, brought about by your crucifixion with Christ?

Romans 8:13–14

Galatians 5:24

Galatians 6:14

Going Deeper

2a. What kinds of habits will help you make daily, moment-by-moment decisions to live the kind of life these passages describe?

DAY 3—RAISED WITH CHRIST

When Paul wanted to talk about the ultimate demonstration of God's power, he chose the resurrection of Christ (Ephesians 1:19–20). This same power of God is able to destroy the great destroyers—sin and death—when we place our faith in Christ and are united with Him in His new life. Now you have the freedom to live fully in the center of God's will. And the adventure ahead of you surpasses anything you can imagine!

> Now you're unlimited in your capacity to present to God everything you do and everything you are, all for *righteousness*.

LESSON

7

DAY

3

Maybe you're thinking, "That's true for some people, but not for me. I can't change."

Remember, if you place your faith in Christ, God says you are a new creation (2 Corinthians 5:17).

LESSON

7

DAY

3

How many of those who enter into a saving relationship with Christ have this change in their life? *Every solitary one!* It isn't negotiable; it isn't an option to consider, but a reality to accept and apply and live by. You become immersed into a relationship with Christ so that you're a new creation, with old things passed away and all things becoming new.

So as you complete this lesson, choose the path of faith—choose to believe that what God says about you is true, though your feelings and experience want to deny it.

Key Question 3

Read again through Romans 6, this time paying special attention to our participation with Christ in His resurrection. In a few sentences, summarize Paul's teaching on this theme.

Going Deeper

3a. What practical guidance for daily living does Colossians 3:1–10 provide?

DAY 4—FREED FOR RIGHTEOUSNESS

Jesus lived sinlessly (Hebrews 4:15; 7:26). Every believer is united with Christ in new life, with new potential for righteous living.

> Those who have been born by the Spirit of God do not continually practice sin because God has placed within you His seed—His Son, and everything about Him. His Son, who dealt radically with sin on the cross, now dwells within you and seeks to live out *His* life in *yours*. Christ living within us now orchestrates our lives to walk free from sin.

Key Question 4

Christ is our sinless model, which God calls us to follow in a life of righteousness. But Christ's role in our righteous living involves more than His example. What and how? (See Romans 5:17–21; 2 Corinthians 5:21.)

Going Deeper

4a. Read how John depicts the Christian's life in 1 John 3:5–10. How can he make such extreme statements?

LESSON

7

DAY

4

LESSON

7

DAY

4

4b. What does your real union with Christ have to do with the life John describes?

> Does that mean we live a perfect life? Does it mean you're completely free from committing any sin? No, but it does mean a consistent pursuit of holiness and consistent growth in holiness. Though we still commit occasional sins, we no longer *continue* in sin; we no longer *remain* in sin. For the person who's truly born again, staying in sin is an impossibility.

DAY 5—OUR NEW GUARDIAN

> There's no such thing as a genuine child of God who isn't indwelt with the Holy Spirit. God the Father has assigned the Holy Spirit to make absolutely certain that He constantly convinces you of sin, because sin is your ruin. Sin holds back everything God has in mind for you.

Key Question 5

How can you learn to listen better and cooperate more as the Holy Spirit does His work in your heart? (See John 16:8–11; 1 Corinthians 2:12–16.)

Going Deeper

5a. How can you tell if you're allowing God's Spirit to do His job in you? (See Galatians 5:22–23; Colossians 3:12–14.)

CONCLUSION—EXPERIENCING THE CROSS

Satan, our lying and deceitful adversary, will tell you, "Come on! You know you sin. You're a sinner. That's what you do. That's what you are. You're going to keep right on sinning."

How do you deal with that mocking, sneering voice? You won't be able to fight it if you are relying on your personal experience to interpret and determine the meaning of Scripture. The only way to deal with it is to take the truth of Scripture and lay it *over* your experience. Bring your experience up to the Word of God!

LESSON

7

DAY

5

When we rely on human wisdom and experience, rather than God's Word, we make His cross of no effect in our lives (1 Corinthians 1:17).

Key Question 6: Reflecting on the Cross

This time, let your prayer be a declaration of the truth God has already revealed. Here is one way that Dr. Blackaby has prayed:

> God's Word says that I'm never again in bondage to sin, and I don't have to sin. So I come again to my Savior to get victory as I present my body as an instrument of righteousness unto God.... I can take those Scriptures and live them out. I now place my full trust in the Holy Spirit to keep me free by the Word of God and the Truth of God.

The best way to reinforce your resolve is to bathe yourself in God's Word. As you continue to pray, write below the truths you most want God to make unshakably real in your mind.

I'm afraid there are many who've never truly turned from their sin, yet believe they are saved. But if they have never dealt with sin in their lives, if they have never repented and turned away from their sin, salvation is impossible....

Have you been radically born from above by letting the Father deal with *your* sin in His Son Jesus, when He laid that sin upon Him on the cross? Have you believed what God says about this, and fully exchanged the sin in your life for the righteousness of Christ?

6a. If your answer to Dr. Blackaby's questions above is no, we urge you to invite the Lord to apply the full effect of the cross to your life. If you say yes to God's gift of forgiveness and power to live righteously, He will make it yours in an instant. The exact words you use aren't as important as the attitude of complete surrender. Here is one way you might ask:

"Lord, I know that I've sinned against You, and that I've been enslaved to sin. I deserve real, eternal death. But I now accept the death of Jesus Christ in my place. Here's my life; it's Yours. Thank You for cleansing me and for uniting me with Christ in His death and His resurrection. Help me receive all You now make available, that I might live for Your glory."

Key Question 7: Changed by the Cross

Choose one specific new way you will, starting this moment, present your body to God as an instrument of righteousness.

> In your relationship to Christ, all the fullness of God is on the inside of you, causing you to present your bodies to God as instruments of righteousness....
>
> Remember that you belong to Him, body and soul, and keep offering yourself to Him hour by hour, moment by moment.

For Meditation and Memorization

For the love of Christ compels us, because we judge thus: that if One died for all, then all died; and He died for all, that those who live should live no longer for themselves, but for Him who died for them and rose again. (2 Corinthians 5:14–15)

For Further Study and Application

- *Our participation in Christ's death and resurrection:* John 14:19; Galatians 6:14; 1 Corinthians 15:20–23; 2 Corinthians 4:8–12; Philippians 3:8–17.

FOLLOWING THE WAY OF THE CROSS

A companion study to chapters 16–18 in
Experiencing the Cross

LIFE CHANGE OBJECTIVES

It is our prayer that after you have finished this lesson...

- You will grow in your trust in God and your surrender to His will.

- You will commit to a lifetime of discipleship under Christ.

- You will complete the event of the cross by taking the message of the cross to those who need it.

DAY 1—THE PATH OF SURRENDER

"Please don't send me to Africa!"

Those were the humorous words of a popular Christian song many years ago. But the song's message reflected a serious fear for millions of Christians: *What if God wants me to go out of my comfort zone?*

Here's news: You can be *certain* that God wants you out of your comfort zone. While He may not send you to Africa, if you'll pay attention, you'll eventually hear Him calling you to something you'll find frightening. But this something may be your life purpose. If so, He will give you everything you need in order to accomplish it, and there's nothing you could do with your life that would give you greater fulfillment.

Why would anyone be willing to give up comfort and security? Because Jesus gave up so much more for us.

> The distance between your comfortable home now and Africa is infinitely small compared to the distance for Christ between the shining glory of God's throne in heaven and the darkness of His death on the cross.

Two thousand years ago, Jesus in the flesh surrendered completely to the Father's will, even though He agonized over what it would cost Him. Today Jesus *within you* is urging, guiding, and empowering you to take up your cross in surrender to the Father's will for you.

> Jesus said, "I have come down from heaven, not to do My own will, but the will of Him who sent Me" (John 6:38). That's the same reason He has come down from heaven to dwell in your life. Doing the Father's will was and is a constant for Him....
>
> The cross represented the will of God for Jesus. In the same way, the cross for you is the will of God that He desires to work out in your life, whatever that may involve. *Your cross is whatever God reveals as His personal will for you.*

Key Question 1

Read Philippians 2:5–8, 12–13. Working *out* your salvation doesn't mean working *for* your salvation. It means bringing your salvation to its practical conclusion. What is God calling you to do, in His power, as you follow Christ's example?

Going Deeper

1a. What emotional barriers does He need to help you overcome? What or who might He use to help you?

LESSON
8

DAY
1

DAY 2—SURRENDER TO SUFFERING

LESSON

8

DAY

2

> I've found that when believers truly understand the cross, it releases them for anything and everything that's on the mind and heart of God in His purpose for them, regardless of the cost....
>
> We so often want to skip the cross and go straight to Pentecost—to avoid the suffering and go straight to spiritual power and testimony and impact. But the cross must come first. Denying of self comes first.

Key Question 2

• How willing are you to suffer as you follow Christ? (See Matthew 10:24; 16:21, 24–25; Acts 5:40–42; Philippians 3:8–11.)

• How does the completeness (or incompleteness) of your understanding of the cross affect your willingness to suffer for Christ?

Going Deeper

2a. What are some practical ways you can remain mindful that surrender to God's will is always worth whatever cost it requires? (How can you come to a more complete understanding of the cross?)

DAY 3—OUR MOTIVATION FOR SURRENDER

If you want to have the fullest impact of the cross in your life, don't be surprised to discover there are few who want to walk that road with you. But don't be discouraged. That fact ought to be confirmation that you're taking the narrow way [Matthew 7:13–14]. If you look to God instead of to people, He'll affirm for you that you're on the right track. And it may be that God intends to use the witness of your walk on the narrow way to bring His presence and power to many others around you....

The Christian is one who chooses to release His life unconditionally to Jesus' right to be Lord.

LESSON
8

DAY
3

Key Question 3

How can you become more deeply, permanently convinced of each of the following, as motivation for surrender?

The love of God—2 Corinthians 5:14–15; 1 John 4:8–11

Hope of eternity—Romans 8:18; 2 Corinthians 4:17–18

> He knows everything about my tomorrows, and His perfect love can never give me second best…. Every directive God gives is always accompanied by His presence and power to enable us to accomplish and carry out His will….

Going Deeper

3a. How do each of the following passages provide further motivation for complete surrender?

Matthew 25:19–21

Philippians 1:20–23

2 Timothy 4:6–8

DAY 4—THE PATH OF DISCIPLESHIP

> The cross shows us how to die to the world's hold
> upon us, and it opens up our understanding for
> walking the path of discipleship, for a lifetime of
> following our Savior and Shepherd....
>
> Without the cross, there is no discipleship....
>
> Yes, there is a cross for us—but that doesn't cancel
> the joy. There's always a resurrection beyond the cross,
> and this is what makes it worth it all after you've been
> faithful to bear the cost and to endure.

Being a disciple of Christ is not a part–time occupation.

Key Question 4

How can you go about making each of the following characteristics of a disciple part of your inner character? (Choose at
least two.)

LESSON
8

DAY
4

Eternal perspective—Matthew 6:19–21; 2 Corinthians
4:16–18

Joyful endurance—Hebrews 12:2–3; 1 Peter 1:6–9

Fervent prayer to know God's will—Romans 12:1–2; Hebrews 5:7–9

Immersion in God's Word—Psalm 119:15–16, 105, 148; Acts 17:11

Going Deeper

4a. Is there something keeping you from committing to a lifetime as a disciple of Christ? If so, what is it? What are God's answers for that barrier?

4b. Read as much of Psalm 119 as you have time for and list the various reasons the Word of God is necessary in the life of Christ's disciple.

DAY 5—THE PATH OF WITNESS
AND MINISTRY

God gave you physical life and all the material, emotional, relational blessings that come with it.

Then, if you chose to become a child of God, He gave you eternal life and all the spiritual blessings that come with it.

Along with all of those amazing gifts, God has entrusted you with a ministry. In fact, your ministry and its fulfillment are part of His reason for creating and saving you.

Key Question 5

Read 2 Corinthians 5:15–21 and, in your own words, write your job description on earth and your motivation for fulfilling it.

How do you suppose He feels when He has redeemed us at the cost of the cross, only to find us saying, "Not Your will, but mine be done"?…

God gave you a ministry of reconciliation. Did you fully accept that when you became a Christian?

LESSON

8

The work of the cross is not complete in our lives until we take the message of the cross to the world.

DAY

5

LESSON

8

DAY

5

If you and I do what He told us to do, then He will do what only He can do in accomplishing His salvation in the lives of those around us....

The measure of grace He has extended to you becomes immediately the measure of grace He wants you to extend to all others who need it. That's the true measure of your understanding of God's grace in saving you. Has it become the immediate standard by which you deal with everyone else?

Going Deeper

5a. Jesus said that we must be *in* the world, but not *of* the world (John 17:14–18). Why is it impossible for us to carry out our ministry of reconciliation if we fail to satisfy either of these conditions?

When you're trying to lead others to faith in Christ, you help them fully understand what they're doing. You help them understand the significance of their sin. You help them know that the wages of sin is death, an eternal separation from God, a death that is inevitable if they don't accept God's only provision. And then comes the good news: God, because He loved you and doesn't want you to experience that death, now calls you to repent of your sin, to have faith in what God has done and now offers you through Jesus Christ.

5b. What will you say next time you explain the message of the cross to someone who needs it?

CONCLUSION—EXPERIENCING THE CROSS

The moment you acknowledge your need and come to Him seeking His provision and releasing your life for Him to work, He'll show you what it means to deny self.

Key Question 6: Reflecting on the Cross

Come to your Lord now with an open mind and heart. Ask for His direction and His reassurance. You might pray something as follows:

"Lord, I acknowledge that You are my Master, and my life belongs to You. Please show me Your purpose for my life, and help me take my selfish purposes out of the way. Thank You for understanding my fears. Along with Your guidance, please give me courage to follow You. Give me constant reminders that Your grace and provision are sufficient, and that no harm or loss will come to me, except what You know I need and can handle."

Use the space below to record your thoughts as you pray.

Some Christians say with frustration, "I prayed, but God didn't hear me," when what they mean is, "God didn't do what I told Him to do." But God doesn't intend to do what you tell Him to do. Prayer isn't designed to get God to do our will; prayer is designed so that we can stand in His presence and know what *His* will is, and submit to it.

And whenever God answers no to your prayers, what you believe about God will be quickly revealed in what you do next. What did Jesus do next? He said, "Not My will, but Thine be done." And He rose up from Gethsemane's ground and submitted to His Father's exact will for Him at that moment, which meant arrest, torture, and the cross.

Key Question 7: Changed by the Cross

What is the next step in God's will for you? Trust Him and step out.

For Meditation and Memorization

For our light affliction, which is but for a moment, is working for us a far more exceeding and eternal weight of glory, while we do not look at the things which are seen, but at the things which are not seen. For the things which are seen are temporary, but the things which are not seen are eternal. (2 Corinthians 4:17–18)

For Further Study and Application

- *The path of surrender:* Matthew 7:13–14; 10:38–39; Luke 13:24; 24:44.

- *The path of discipleship:* Matthew 8:19–22; Matthew 10.

- *The path of witness and ministry:* Matthew 28:18–20; Acts 1:8; Romans 1:16–17.

LEADER'S GUIDE

As you join with others to learn more about the cross of Christ, remember that the Scriptures are your trustworthy textbook and the Holy Spirit Himself is your faithful Teacher. You can be confident that He will lead you into truth (John 16:13).

Here are a few foundational dynamics involved in group study and group discussion to keep in mind as you use this study guide to learn together about the cross:

- The Scriptures are your textbook—not only the passages listed in this study guide, but also other passages the Lord will lead you to as you are open to His guidance.

- The Holy Spirit is your teacher. Be assured that He wants to reveal Himself and His ways to your life. He will instruct you through the Scriptures and also through each person in your group.

- As the Spirit reveals His truth to you, God will require adjustments from each of you. Obediently following through with these adjustments is the key to experiencing God's great salvation in your life.

As the group's leader, spend time considering how these factors should influence the way your group functions.

GROUND RULES

When you first get together, consider asking the group members to agree to the following guidelines to help everyone get the most out of this group study experience.

- Talk about making a commitment to be learners *together* and to be encouraging supporters of one another in this learning process. This study will challenge every group member over strongly held, bedrock assumptions about who we are and what life is about. God's truth about the cross holds potential for revolutionary life change. But many people will be willing to take such daring steps of growth only in a setting where they feel safe. Make a group commitment to lovingly accept each other.

- Encourage each group member to do his or her best to complete all seven Key Questions in each week's lesson.

- Encourage everyone in the group to read through Henry Blackaby's book *Experiencing the Cross.* The corresponding chapters in that book are listed at the beginning of each of lesson. In most cases, this will involve reading two or three chapters for each lesson.

YOUR PREPARATION

As the group's leader, pray diligently about your responsibilities and for all the group members by name. Pray for the Holy Spirit to speak to all of you during your personal study time as well as during your discussion time together.

For all the participants, ask for supernatural blessings from the Holy Spirit and spiritual insight into eternal truths.

Ask for personal discoveries and breakthroughs where these are most needed in your lives.

Ask for protection from disunity, selfishness, and pride; ask for growth together in unity, servanthood, and humility.

As you study and prepare each week, consider writing out in this guide's page margins the text for several key Scripture passages the group will be looking at. This is a good exercise in becoming more familiar with the passages, and it will also mean that the text for them will be immediately at hand during your discussion time.

You will also find additional insight and help by looking up the passages listed in the section titled "For Further Study and Application" at the end of each week's lesson.

Review all of the questions in each week's lesson and decide ahead of time which ones you think are the most important to discuss. We've chosen each lesson's seven Key Questions as our suggestions for the most important, but you know the members of your group, and you are free to choose what you believe is most important for them.

GROUP DISCUSSION

Remember to include prayer as you begin your group discussion—not a token "Bless our time together," but a sincere request for the Holy Spirit to guide your discussion and your learning of the Father's will and purposes. Expect God's Spirit to be in control.

At some point in each week's session, allow for a time of group prayer when all the members are free to communicate with the Lord about the things you're learning together. Suggestions for prayer are included in Key Question 6 of each lesson.

In the discussion, take the lead in sharing honestly from your own life. This will help encourage the others to do so as well. Talk about what you're learning, or still trying to learn, about the lesson. Keep the discussion focused on God's commands and purposes and on your personal application of them.

Here are week-by-week suggestions for life-changing discussions:

LESSON 1: YOUR DESPERATE NEED FOR THE CROSS

This Lesson's Key Thoughts

The cross is not only Christ's, but ours. It is not merely a doctrine to be understood, but a reality to be experienced. It is not just a single historical event; it is at the heart of God's eternal plan. It was not one option among many; it was the only way for God to fulfill His plan. The cross is all about death due to sin—sin that God takes so seriously that He sacrificed the priceless life of His sinless Son in order to deal with it at its root.

Suggestions for Your Discussion

You might begin by reading aloud the following assertion from the introduction of *Experiencing the Cross* and inviting your group to respond to it:

> Too many of God's people are going through life
> missing most of what their Father in heaven intends for
> them to experience, and an inadequate grasp of the
> cross lies at the heart of this tragedy.

Ask your group, "What aspects of God's intended experience do many Christians miss out on? How might these result from an inadequate understanding of the cross?"

Key Question 1: You might take time in your group to pray along these lines together. This might be most effective at the close of your discussion time, but any time is fine.

Key Question 2: You can use this question to establish at the outset that group members should expect this study to change their lives. Encourage your people to personalize their answers instead of talking about Christians in general.

Key Question 3: Failure to recognize the cross as the only way to fulfill God's plan tends to trivialize the cross in our minds. Use this question to help your group recognize this tendency in some of their thinking. Work toward a group determination to remain more mindful of the cross's centrality and necessity.

Key Question 4: Your group will have many opportunities throughout this study to confront the seriousness of sin and the severity of its consequences. Help them to start thinking in that direction, because this theme is central to the cross's meaning.

Key Question 5: This question introduces another theme that will arise later in this study—namely, the concept that at salvation, God didn't just forgive us, but He really changed us. Christians tend to let their discouraging experience cause them to disbelieve that they're truly different. Help your people to challenge these assumptions, taking God's Word at face value.

Key Questions 6 and 7: You might divide your group into same-gender partnerships to share answers to these application questions. Then ask partners to call each other during the week for accountability and encouragement.

As time allows, we suggest questions 2a, 5a, and 6a for additional group discussion.

LESSON 2: THE FATHER'S LOVE IN THE CROSS

This Lesson's Key Thoughts

The Father was as much a party to the cross as was the Son, and He also suffered greatly on our behalf. Sin requires the shedding of blood—that is, the sacrifice of a life. The sacrifice of Jesus' lifeblood was foreshadowed throughout the Old Testament, and we now commemorate it in the Lord's Supper.

Suggestions for Your Discussion

You might start your group discussion by asking, "Who suffered in order that you might be forgiven and receive eternal life?" If people provide only one-word answers, prompt them to explain or support their answers. After a few minutes of discussion, transition into Key Questions 1 and 2, if the group hasn't already begun to address them.

Key Question 1: This question focuses on the Father's *planning for* and *participation in* the cross, whereas Key Question 2 addresses His *suffering* in the cross. Your group very likely will merge discussions of the two. This is fine, because the two are simply different aspects of the same phenomenon.

Key Question 2: As you discuss this, it might be helpful to remind your group that, although the relationship between the Father and the Son is similar in some respects to a human father-son relationship, there are aspects of their relationship that are also quite different, and we can't fully understand it. When we encounter these inscrutable areas of God's nature, eventually we can respond only with gratitude and worship.

Key Question 3: The bottom line is that blood equals life. A sacrifice of blood implies a fatality.

Key Question 4: Help your people consider such specifics as the animal's perfect spotlessness, the fact that participation was available to anyone, the animal's necessary death, the ceremony's protection against death, God's combat against the gods of Egypt, and the command never to forget this ceremony.

Key Question 5: Our celebration of Communion is enriched when we bring in the intentional symbolism of the Passover, along with the new insights Jesus added—especially the clarification that Israel had always been celebrating the breaking of His body and the outpouring of His blood.

Key Questions 6 and 7: You might close your discussion time with group prayer and worship around Isaiah 53. Again, we suggest same-gender accountability partners for follow-up on specific commitments people make.

As time allows, we suggest questions 2a and 2b for additional group discussion, as this will prepare the way for a richer experience in Key Question 6.

LESSON 3: THE SON'S OBEDIENCE IN THE CROSS

This Lesson's Key Thoughts
God the Son obeyed His Father perfectly, giving up rights that He deserved to keep, even through much suffering, even to the point of a death that is beyond our comprehension. He did this both as our example to follow and as our substitute, that we might never have to experience true death.

Suggestions for Your Discussion
The focus of this lesson is on our comprehension of Christ's complete obedience and the true death He died. But it's also appropriate to examine ways we can follow His example of obedience, because our obedience should be the natural result of these truths, as well as our most fitting worship of our Savior. Plan for a two-pronged emphasis—comprehension and imitation of Jesus' obedience.

Key Question 1: This question is intended to help your people take Jesus' perfect obedience out of the realm of abstract concept and bring it into tangible reality.

Key Question 2: For most Christians, the idea that Jesus had to learn obedience and had to be made complete or mature seems to imply that He had previously sinned. But there's a difference between overcoming sin and growing into maturity. When we grasp this, we actually find ourselves identifying even more closely with Jesus' challenges throughout His life—even as an adult. He wasn't ready for the cross until He had gone through every experience that led up to it.

Key Question 3: Jesus' suffering on our behalf did not start on the cross, but long before the cross, when He left heaven's glory.

Key Question 4: Imagine you're peering down into a chasm so deep that the bottom is hidden in darkness. Even though you can't see the bottom, you're impressed with its depth. Similarly, even though true children of God will never know by experience the ultimate horror of spiritual death, we must gaze down into its depths in order that we might more gratefully worship Him who endured its full impact.

Key Question 5: Invite your group to commit together always to speak of Jesus' death with its true magnitude in mind.

Key Questions 6 and 7: As your people choose specific ways they'll follow Jesus' example of obedience, help them realize that they're expressing gratitude and worship to Him by their obedience.

As time allows, we suggest questions 3b and 5a for additional group discussion.

LESSON 4: THE WORK ACCOMPLISHED ON THE CROSS

This Lesson's Key Thoughts

Jesus, the sinless one, truly became sin on the cross. And we, the sinful ones, can truly become the righteousness of God in Christ. Because of our identification with the cross, where this exchange was made possible, we are now transformed and united with Christ against sin. The event of the cross was completed by Christ's resurrection, which confirmed the acceptability of His sacrifice.

Suggestions for Your Discussion

Even after completing a study like this one, many Christians find these concepts simply too fantastic to be true. You can prepare your group to break through this belief barrier by discussing at the outset the difference between fantasy and truth, and the fact that God has indeed made this dream a reality.

Key Question 1: The purpose for this question is to help your people take a fresh look at familiar passages, discovering in them the startling truth that belongs there. You might need to help them do this.

Key Question 2: As you discuss these benefits, the purpose of the question is partly to help your people understand the incomprehensible price God paid to make them ours. The outcome in our lives should be that we stop taking these benefits for granted.

Key Question 3: The idea of our participation in Christ's crucifixion will be emphasized in greater depth in later lessons. Use this question to help your people begin to think about the fact that our "death to sin" is real.

Key Question 4: This question can help your people gain greater confidence as they face difficulties. But it also serves as a lead-in to Key Question 5, which gets closer to the heart of the matter for purposes of this lesson. Unless your people need to dwell on this, we recommend that you move quickly to the next section of the lesson.

Key Question 5: Another way of coming at this is to ask, "Why is the event of the cross incomplete without Christ's resurrection?" The question as it's worded in the lesson helps your people personalize the resurrection for themselves, and it helps them accept it as a real, historic event.

Key Questions 6 and 7: At this point in the study series, you're about to begin the lessons that focus on the believer's experience of the cross. These questions are meant to help your group members own their identification with the cross, so that its established reality in them can have a greater impact on their daily lives. Encourage them in this practical direction. And keep motivating them by reinforcing the truth of the exchange of our sin for God's righteousness.

As time allows, we suggest questions 1a, 2a, and 3b for additional group discussion.

LESSON 5: NEW DOORS OPENED
BY THE CROSS

This Lesson's Key Thoughts

When God applies the cross to our lives, we are genuinely transformed into new creations, given access to everything we need, and presented with an accomplished victory over Satan and evil.

Suggestions for Your Discussion

This lesson covers many topics. Feel free to spend a little time on each, but we suggest that you choose one of the three main themes for the focus of your group's discussion—our genuine transformation (Days 1–3), our complete provision (Day 4), or our accomplished victory (Day 5). This limited focus will allow your group to gain greater depth of understanding and to go further with personal application. Later they can come back and dig deeper into the other topics.

Key Question 1: All of us have some degree of difficulty accepting that we are genuinely transformed. We encourage you to tell your people this to help them feel safer about discussing their individual challenges to belief.

Key Question 2: Sometime setting a falsehood next to a truth makes the nature of both more apparent.

Key Question 3: Keep the focus on the fact that Paul was writing about changes that are *real*, not just theologically abstract and fanciful. It will probably help to discuss the outward signs in the life of a person who lets these real changes shine through. The limiting factor is our confidence in the changes, not in whether or not they are real.

Key Question 4: You might distribute these passages to different group members before your meeting, letting individuals share with the rest of the group what they've learned.

Key Question 5: Once again, the goal here is to help your group members believe in the truth of Christ's victory over evil. Even though He has won, we lose when Satan successfully convinces that we've lost. The difference is all in our perspective.

Key Questions 6 and 7: No one can reverse a lifetime of disbelief or inaccurate understanding in a single day or week. Therefore, one important task for your group is to help each other develop a lifelong habit of praying along the lines of Dr. Blackaby's sample prayer. We suggest that you pray together for increased understanding and fuller appropriation of God's many gifts. Then hold each other accountable to pray this way daily for at least a month.

As time allows, we suggest questions 2a and 4a for additional group discussion.

LESSON 6: VIEWING SIN IN LIGHT OF THE CROSS

This Lesson's Key Thoughts

Taking up our cross means actively cooperating with God's radical dealing with our sin. The Christian who won't do this can't be a disciple of Christ. Sin is deadly, even for Christians, and we must take it as seriously as God does. Sin affects others around us. We deal with sin by prompt and complete repentance.

Suggestions for Your Discussion

You might start out your discussion with a graphic illustration of sin's destructive effect. Take some object of genuine value—a beautiful painting, for example—and destroy it in front of the group. You might start out by inflicting small degrees of damage to show the way that "small" sins add up. But then one devastating blow or slash can show also the capacity of sin to cause sudden and irreparable harm. Invite your group to discuss the variety of ways this happens in human lives and relationships.

Key Question 1: Western Christians have learned to rationalize and excuse. Jesus' stark contrasts should wake us up to the need for a zero-tolerance policy with our sin. That doesn't mean we set aside grace and forgiveness, but it does mean that we stop ignoring the damage that sin unavoidably causes.

Key Question 2: The word *disciple* means "learner." Christ calls us always to remain in His classroom, continually asking, "What's the next lesson for me, Lord?" When we step out of His classroom, we don't cease to be God's children, but we do cease to be disciples. We need to get back in school.

Key Question 3: For a Christian, sin's deadly effects can include physical illness and death, death of marriages and other relationships, death of dreams and opportunities, and so on.

Key Question 4: In our individualistic society, we have lost touch with the reality that we aren't islands. Even Christians often think, "If it doesn't hurt anyone else, it's okay." But sin always hurts others. Use this question to help your people acknowledge the corporate solidarity of families, communities, nations, and other groupings of people.

Key Question 5: The Greek word for *repent* literally means to "change one's mind." But we've refrained from saying this in the lesson because although true repentance starts with a change of mind, it never stops there. It must result in changed behavior to be proven genuine. That's the common thread in all of the passages in this question.

Key Questions 6 and 7: Although it is harmful to force group members to share with the group anything they consider too sensitive, we urge you to explain that members need to share their new commitments with *someone*. So ask everyone to tell a partner in the group *the name of a person* they will share their new commitments with (maybe a spouse or a close friend outside the group).

As time allows, we suggest questions 2a, 3a, and 5a for additional group discussion.

LESSON 7: LIVING IN THE POWER
OF THE CROSS

This Lesson's Key Thoughts
A believer is actually united with Christ in His death, and therefore freed from sin. And the believer is actually united with Christ in His resurrection, and therefore freed for righteousness. The Holy Spirit ministers within us, convicting us of sin; we see evidence of His success in our lives by the "fruit" that we bear.

Suggestions for Your Discussion

The study of Romans 6 (Days 1 and 3) is central to this lesson. Your group would profit greatly if you spent all of your discussion time in this chapter.

Key Question 1: We suggest you invite group members to highlight verses that stand out to them. If they need direction, you might focus on verses 1–7, 12–13, 20–23.

Key Question 2: Paul used graphic wording in each of these passages in order to startle us into a fresh understanding of our death to sin. He also emphasizes our active participation in making this reality evident in our conduct.

Key Question 3: As in Key Question 1, invite your people to share from favorite verses. Or you might focus on verses 4–5, 8–10, 13, 18, 22.

Key Question 4: Christ's sinless example is important for us. But He also lives in us, has transformed us (so that we are now able *not* to sin), and guides and empowers us.

Key Question 5: We are able to numb our consciences. This happens as we continually excuse sin, and several group members may have already-numbed consciences. Discuss ways to re-sensitize one's conscience. This could include praying for God to cause this change, developing the habits of reading Scripture and actively listening to God, and inviting accountability and feedback from others (and listening nondefensively).

Key Questions 6 and 7: Invite your members to share with the group one safe-to-share truth that they would like to embed in their minds and hearts. Have someone write up a list of these so that the group can pray for each other. Consider using same-gender accountability partners to follow up on commitments in question 7.

Question 6a: Keep your eyes and ears open for signs that anyone in your group might be uncertain of his or her salvation. Don't assume that all of your group members truly understand the gospel. If appropriate, talk with the individual privately to clarify the gospel or to allow Scripture to provide assurance of salvation.

As time allows, we suggest questions 2a, 3a, and 5a for additional group discussion.

LESSON 8: FOLLOWING THE WAY
OF THE CROSS

This Lesson's Key Thoughts
Just as Jesus surrendered to the Father's will, so must we. And just as Jesus suffered in His obedience, we must expect the same. But when we understand the cross, we welcome surrender at any cost, because we become confident of God's love and of the hope of eternity. Taking up our cross means a lifetime as Christ's disciple. We complete the event of the cross by taking the message of the cross to those who need it.

Suggestions for Your Discussion
This is the "home stretch" lesson. While it will introduce new ideas and applications, invite each of your people to bring the entire series to a point by focusing in on one application from anywhere in the series.

This should be the direction in which each person directs his or her prayer, growth, and obedience over the next few weeks. Plan to set up ongoing accountability in some form.

Key Question 1: Because this question may naturally lead to a discussion of the cost of surrender, you might want to discussion this and Key Question 2 at the same time.

Key Question 2: Emphasize that understanding the cross is the key to willing surrender and sacrifice. That's why prayerful reading and meditation on Scripture is critical to a life in God's will.

Key Question 3: These motives for surrender are also reinforced by time in God's Word. Don't be afraid to point this out often in your discussion.

Key Question 4: The key concept in this section of the lesson is *lifelong* discipleship. Each of the four characteristics will all support longevity as a disciple.

Key Question 5: We suggest that you take time to discuss the quotes from *Experiencing the Cross* that immediately follow Key Question 5. Ask your group, "What most effectively motivates you to share the message of the cross with others?"

Key Questions 6 and 7: See "Suggestions for Your Discussion" above. Encourage members to choose one long-term application from anywhere in the series.

As time allows, we suggest questions 2a, 4a, and 5a for additional group discussion.

From Henry and Mel Blackaby

Find out from Henry and Mel Blackaby how spiritual gifts work for the common good of the body of Christ—and learn where you fit in.

What's So Spiritual About Your Gifts?
ISBN 1-59052-344-X
US $9.99

Multnomah® Publishers *Keeping Your Trust…One Book at a Time*®

From Henry Blackaby

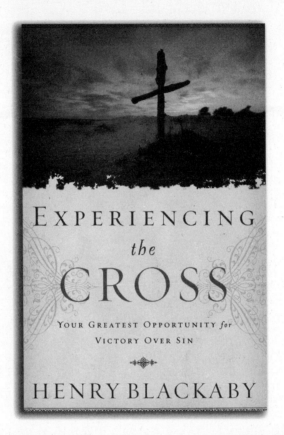

Blackaby swings wide the door to an intense experience with God while coming to understand the deeper dimensions of the cross.

Experiencing the Cross
ISBN 1-59052-480-2
US $16.99

Multnomah® Publishers *Keeping Your Trust...One Book at a Time*®

From Henry Blackaby

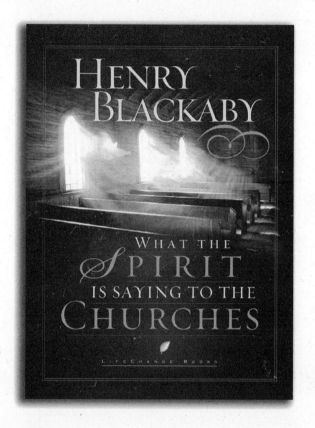

Bestselling author Henry Blackaby teaches church laypeople how to stay sensitive to the Holy Spirit's ever-fresh guidance—and fulfill their congregation's unique mission.

What the Spirit Is Saying to the Churches
ISBN 1-59052-036-X
US $9.99